AF374798

Yes!
No.
Maybe?

Yes!
No.
Maybe?

three little words
that change everything

Barbara A. Berger

Illustrated by Brent Pettit

Live Your Genuine

Live Your Genuine books may be ordered from your favorite bookseller.
www.LiveYourGenuine.com

First edition
Hardcover 7x10: 979-8-9930985-1-7
Hardcover 8x10: 979-8-9930985-3-1
Paperback 8x10: 979-8-9930985-2-4
Kindle also available.

Library of Congress Cataloging Number 2025920407
Cataloging-in-Publication data on file with publisher.

Publishing and production by Concierge Publishing Services
Printed in the United States of America
10 9 8 7 6 5 4 3 2 1

For my family...blood and not. The ones here
and just over there. I'm so glad you said Yes!

YES!

(a divine deal)

There once was a Light

A big Light all alone

It was big, It was bright

And, oh my, how It shone

Way before stars

And before the sun

It was alone out there

The only Light...the only one

Some call It God,

The Divine, Source, or Love

And It started all things

Below and above

The Light asked a question

To Itself—or so it seemed

And answers echoed back

From near and far and in between

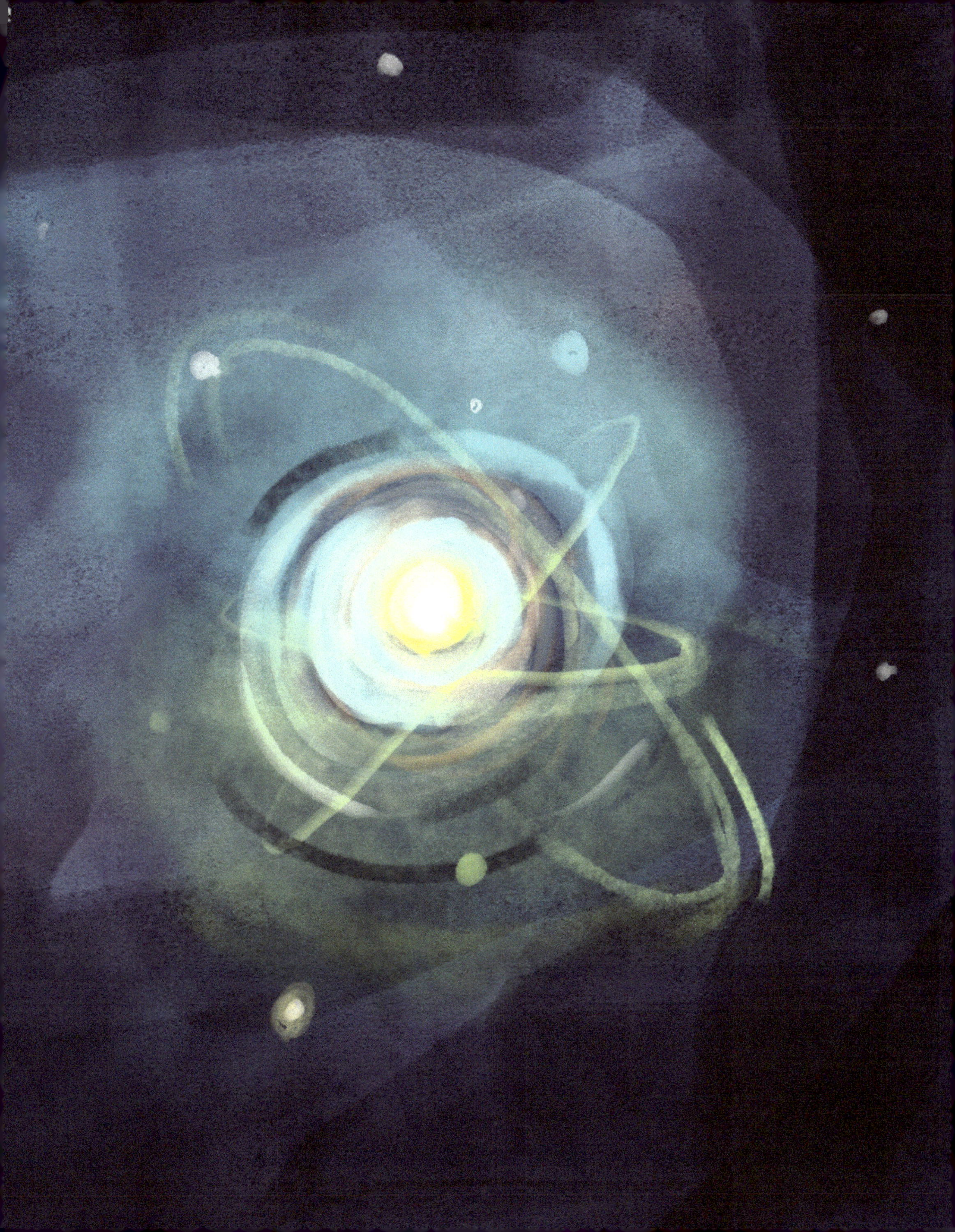

What question did the big Light ask?
What was it, you must wonder

"If there is only one of Me,
would you be the other?"

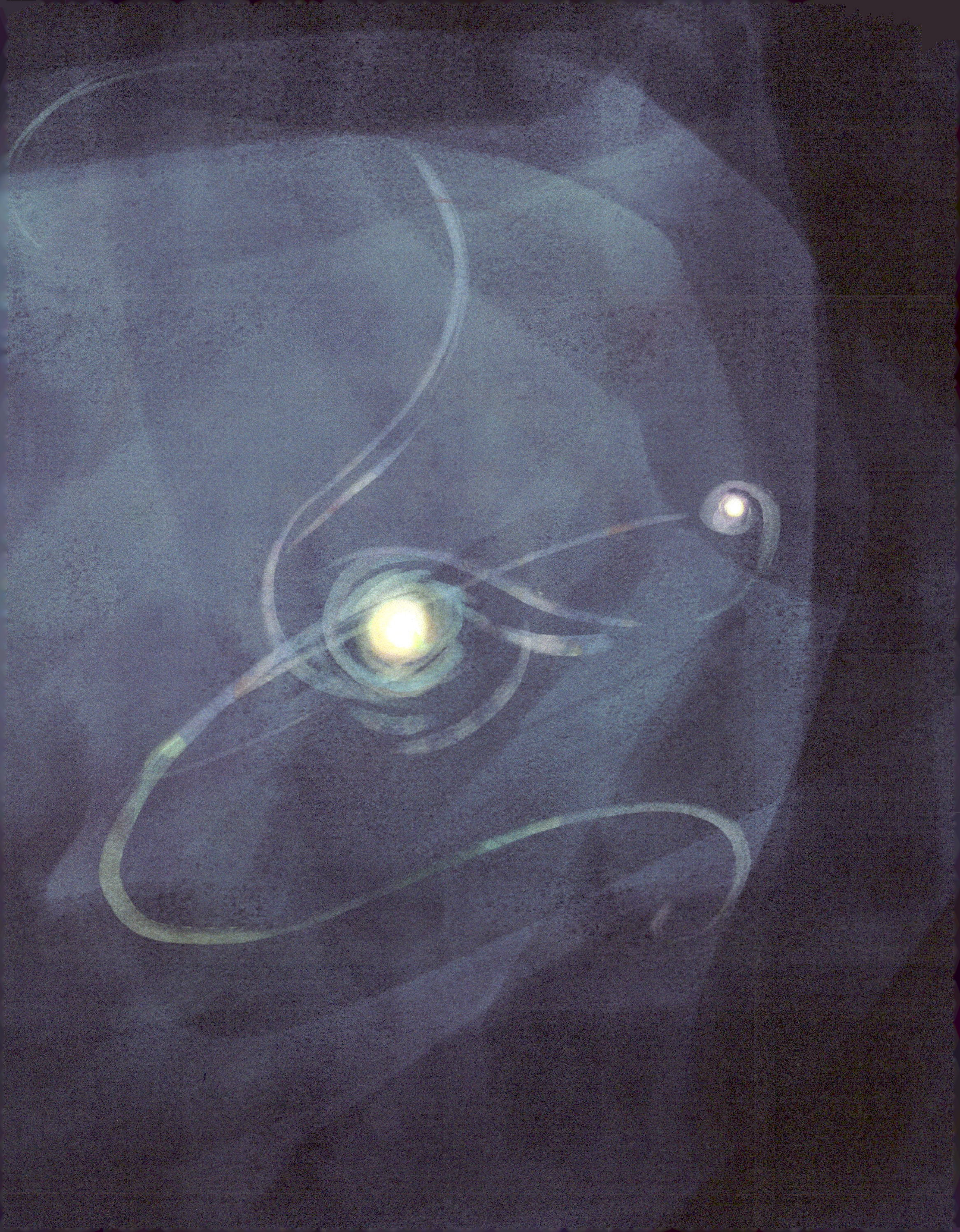

That question started all that is

From planets to the trees

It was answered with a loving Yes

From everything you see

A Yes came from your family

From your dog, and from cats, too

A Yes came from the sun and stars

And a big Yes! came from you

To what, exactly,

Did you agree so very long ago?

To be a Spark of God's bright Light

Everywhere you go

If I am only one big Light,

and I share my Light with you,

then you will be a part of Me

and you'll have a job to do.

I'm asking that you shine so bright

This Light I give to you

Reminding others as you glow

They have the same Light, too

So practice each day

Seeing Light in all things

From the grass to the trees

To the hornet that stings

Because Yes! said sisters,
Brothers, fathers, and mothers
Yes! said the humans of every color

Yes! said the weary, the sick, and the sad
So, look for the Light,
It's the same Light you have

Use It always to help those who forgot
That the Spark I gave you
Is the same Spark they got

While our outsides look different
Inside we're the same
When you look at the other
Remember again

You're looking at Me
And you're looking at you
My same Light in everything
So pure and so true

It can get covered up
Sometimes It goes dim
And sometimes it's so hard
To believe It's in them...

The bullies, the meanies
The ones who forget
To treat others as Light
Even though they said Yes

I promise you this

Dear one, from my heart

We're all from one Light

We're not ever apart

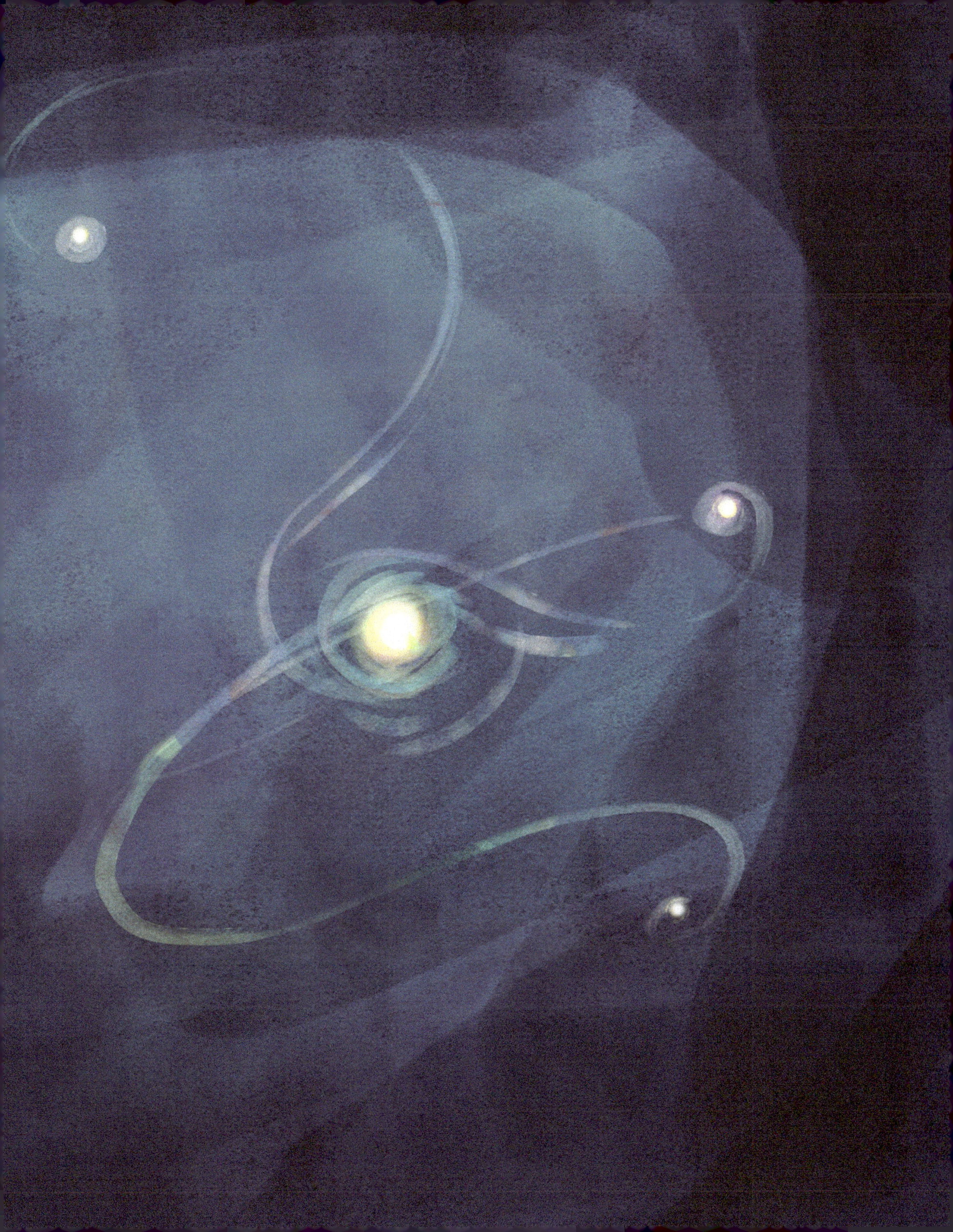

No longer alone

The Source Light can see

All that was made

From Its Love energy

So happy It shared

The Light you possess

And so very happy you answered with...

YES!

NO.
(for days when you forget)

I know I said No
There's no way that I didn't
I didn't say Yes—
There's no way you can spin it

If God ever asked
If I'd carry Its light
I must've said No
I don't ever shine bright

I'm just a mistake

I hear what they say

When they whisper and laugh

As I walk away

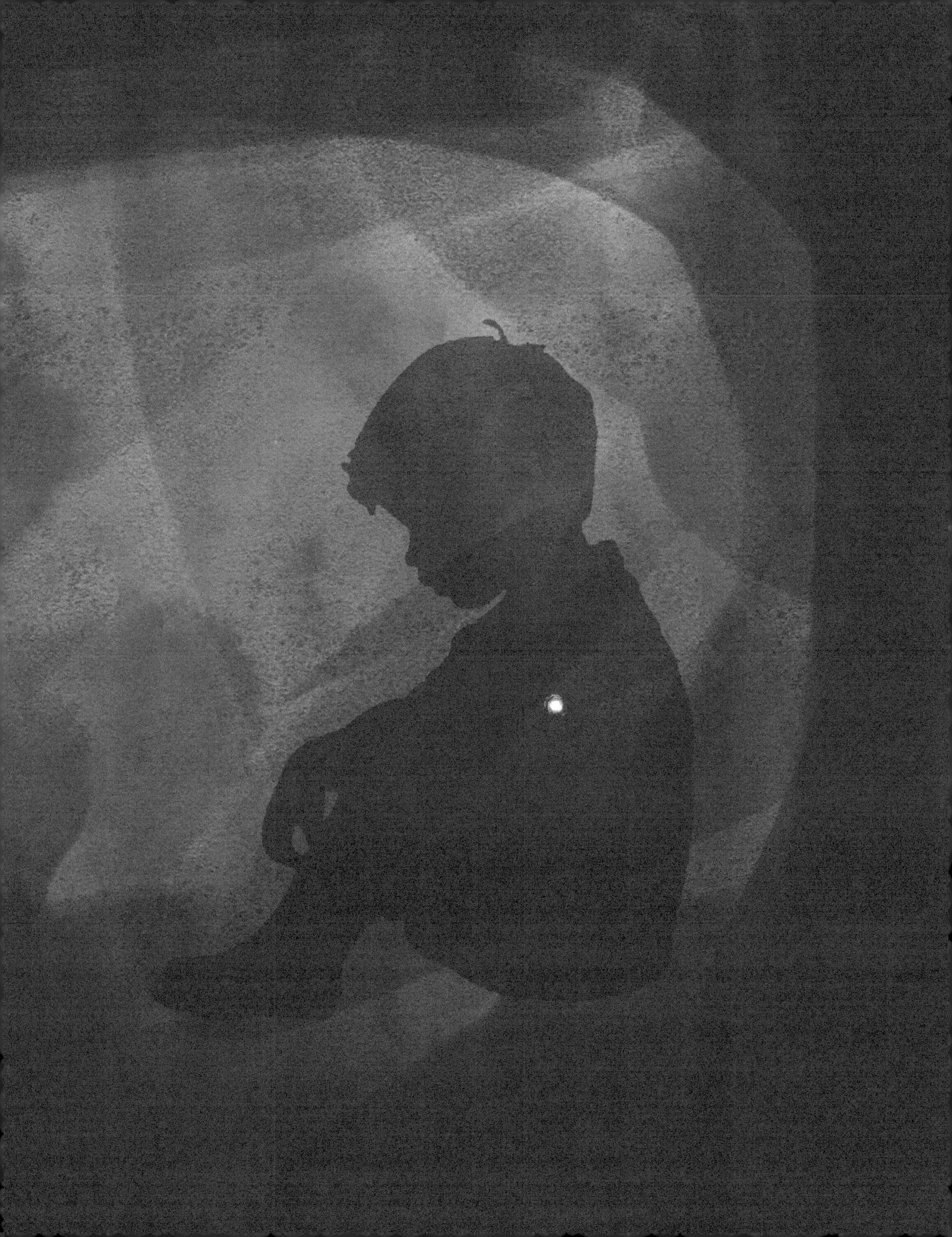

My arms are too skinny

My nose is too long

My hair is too frizzy

My teeth are all wrong

I'm too big

I'm too small

I'm too smart

I'm too tall

I'm too different, too odd

I'm nothing at all

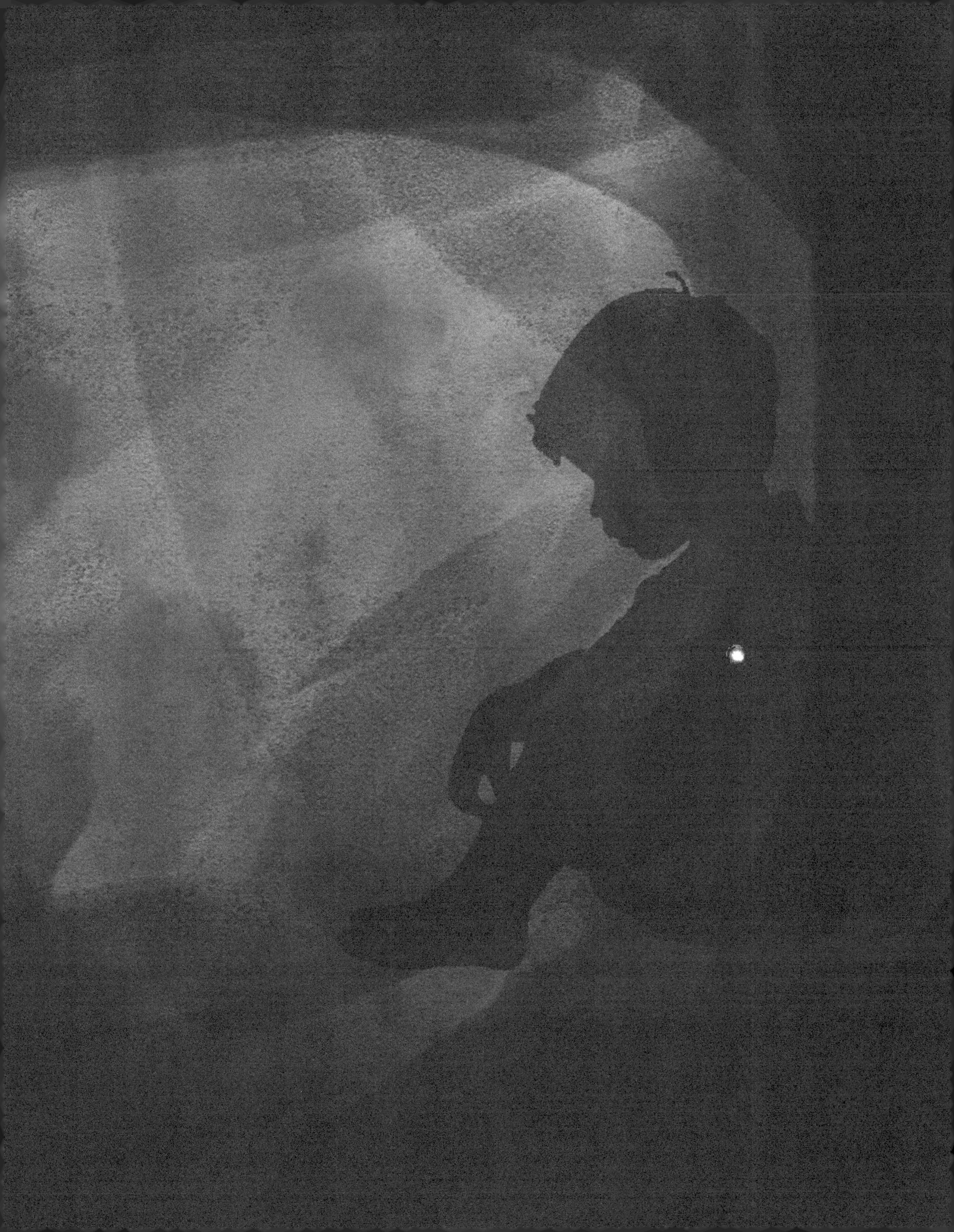

No, no, there's no way

It can possibly be

That a spark of God's Light

Lives inside of me

I don't have a Light

I don't have a shine

I mess up a lot

I'm imperfect sometimes

So, if Source ever asked

If I'd carry Its Light

I must've said No

I don't ever shine bright

Now wait just a minute,

You heard a voice say

You seem to believe

That I made a mistake

I didn't mess up

And I didn't guess

I gave my Love Light

To the ones who said Yes

There will be days

When you can't find your glow

It may seem you don't have one

But I need you to know

That the No you're so sure

That you said to Me

You can use for yourself

More powerfully

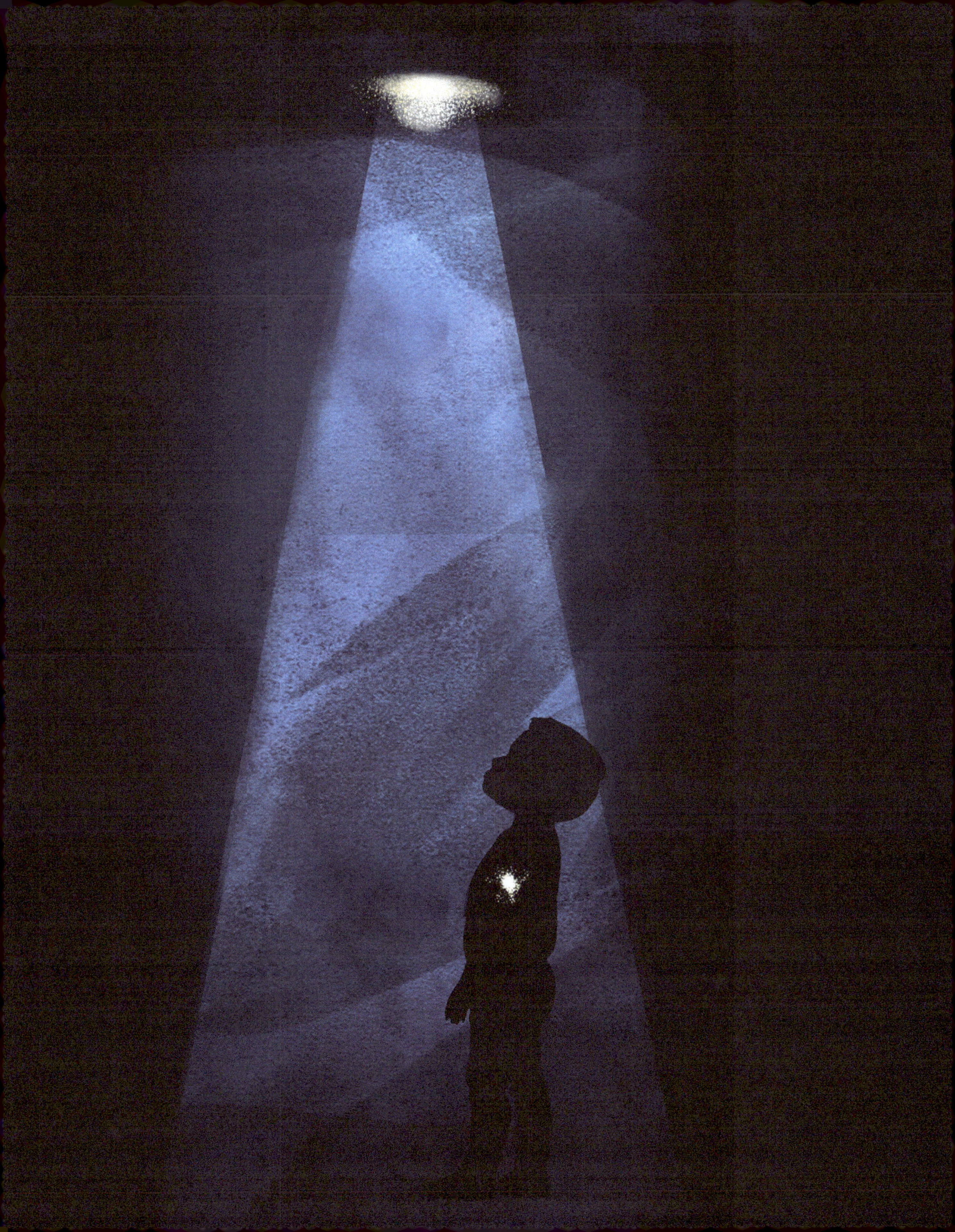

Your No is your armor
Your No is your shield
Your No is a superpower
That you can wield

And say No to the whispers
That tell you you're less
Say No to the lies that
Make you feel stress

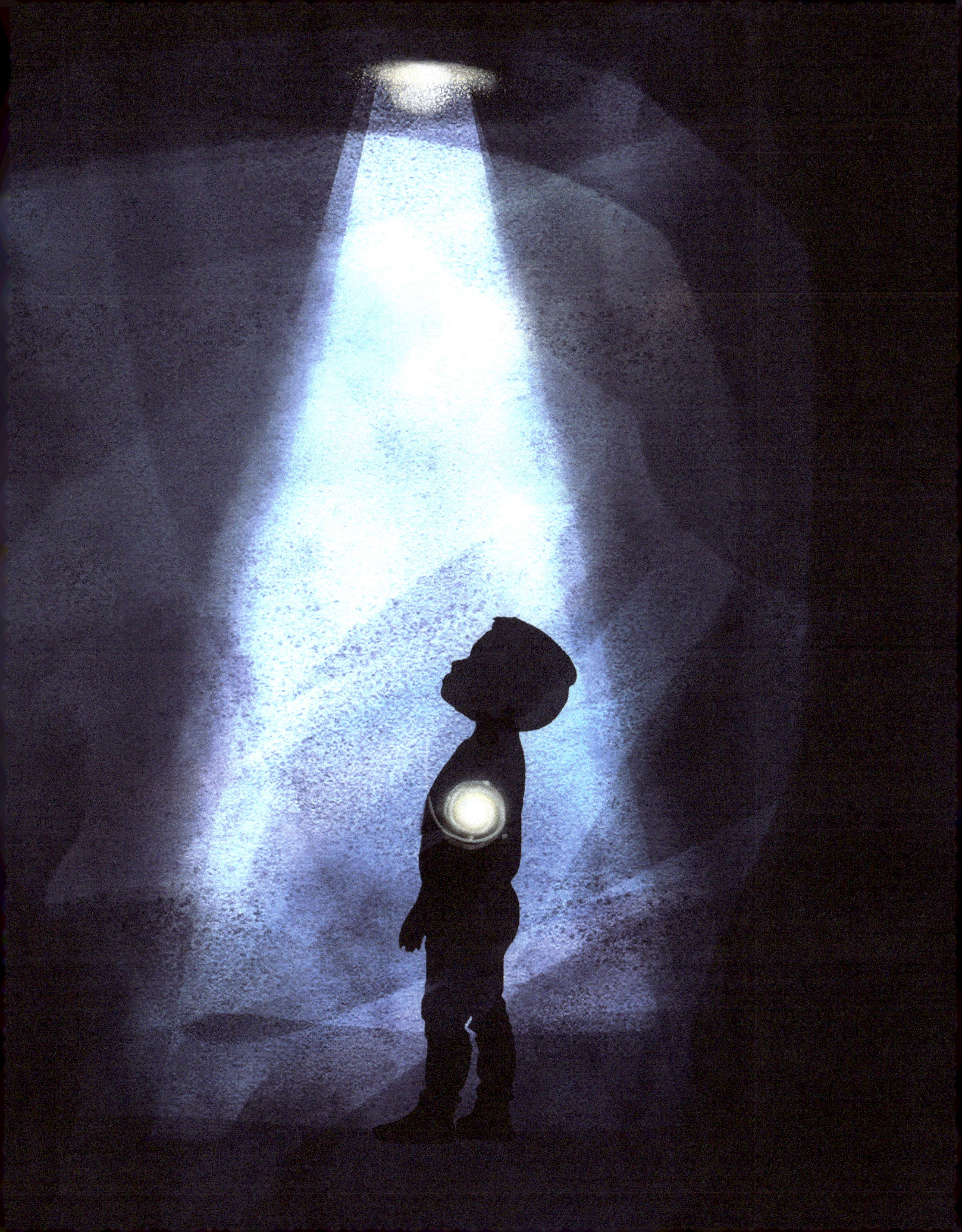

Your No is your guide

To help you be real

To own who you are

And own how you feel

The No that you need

Is a No to the downers

And the negative thoughts

That zap your Light's power

Challenge those thoughts
About the things others say
When you start to believe
You were made some wrong way

You wouldn't be here
If you hadn't said Yes
You're a Spark of Source Light
Perfectly blessed

You'll have all kinds of feelings
You'll have days that feel low
So talk about them
It's good to do that, you know

Once you've felt all the feels
And thought them all through
You get to decide
What's most helpful for you

Choose which ones to keep

And which ones to let go

Which ones to cast out

With the power of No

Your No is your secret

So your bright self

Can shine through

Because you said Yes to Me...

And I said

Yes!

to you!

MAYBE?

(a way back to Yes)

Think how important
A Maybe can be
It's a magical word
Did you know

Those five little letters
Arranged in that way
Hold power...
Like Yes and like No

It's about what you try

When you find yourself stuck

In a No kind of day

And you're feeling like yuck

Source Light is still there

Even though you think not

And trying a Maybe

Can show what you've got

Think to yourself
"Maybe if I _____________"
Then fill in the blank
And you may be surprised

Just look at the world and all that you see
The trees, the oceans, the sky—
They came from a Maybe, so long ago
When God thought, "Maybe I'll try."

You may think it's crazy
But I tell you it's true
The magic of Maybe
Works the same way for you

Maybe is brave
Maybe is strong
Maybe says
"Try, and see what comes along"

What do you like?

What gives you spunk?

What are some of the

Thoughts that you've thunk?

I'd like to do this

Or I want to try that

Or this makes me happy

Or I wonder about that

The Maybe that gives you a jolt full of joy

This is the one to try first

Because joy is a signal of Source energy

So follow that energy burst

Maybe I could draw or paint

Or dance or sing a tune

Maybe I could ride my bike

Or rearrange my room

Maybe I could learn that thing

I've always wondered about

Maybe I could take a walk

Or help somebody out...

Just like Yes and like No

The words we use shape our way

How you talk to yourself matters so much

It can brighten or darken your day

Maybe nudges you gently

It helps you to see

How the Light in you

Can create beautifully

A Maybe can take you

One step ahead

Out of your worries

Out of your head

Follow your Maybe

Make It your guide

Let It show you

Your true Spark inside

If you never play Maybe

You may never know

What feeds your energy

And makes your Light grow

What will you try?

What will you do?

Maybe holds magic

That's waiting for you

Some will work out

Some never do

But all Maybes you try

Give you clues about you

Your Light is unique

Your Light will shine best

When you trust that your Maybes

Will lead to your

YES!

About the Author

Barbara A. Berger, PCC, is a career and executive coach and founder of Career Wellness Partners and Live Your Genuine Coaching.

The line, "If there is only one of me, would you be the other?" arrived as a download a decade before this book. Its meaning didn't click until late 2024, while she was deep into writing a different book about work and career coaching. That moment sparked an instant pivot from client case studies to soul contracts.

It's what wanted to happen.

She's built a life, and a business, on helping people trust their gut, follow their curiosity, and answer the call their logical brain keeps trying to shush. She believes in the magic of following the intuitive whisper...because the good stuff starts where the plan ends. • LiveYourGenuine.com • YesNoMaybeBook.com

About the Illustrator

Brent Pettit is an illustrator from Sioux Falls, SD. His passion for drawing began in childhood and became his full-time career in 2018. Inspired by laughter, he uses his art as a way to understand and share his unique perspective on the world. When he's not creating, he enjoys spending time with his wife and four children, playing music, reading, cooking, and exploring the world of Dungeons & Dragons.

Acknowledgments

So much gratitude goes to Lisa Pelto, my editor and sherpa throughout this process. To Erin Pankowski, for her endless patience while translating such an abstract vision, especially when I couldn't see it clearly myself. And thank you, Brent Pettit, for not bailing when the vision shape-shifted (repeatedly).

Thank you to the vibrant group of souls who steady, inspire, and challenge me. I'm so grateful for each of you.

To my mom, dad and Mark: Thank you. Thank you. Thank you.

Thank you to Derek, my chemist-husband, for enduring my right-brained antics. I'm glad you're you. And to Michael and Alec...you know that you're my entire heart. May you always feel safe to connect, create, and build lives that are peaceful, joyful, and wildly your own. Thank you for choosing me as your mom.

And to Choncho, our soul dog of 16.5 years. The countless hours on the couch with you during those last few months opened space for this book to pour out. Thank you for saying Yes to us.